The Seven Challenges of Value

Discover the secrets of customer value, build your revenue, improve your margin and enjoy a lot more profit...

Mike Wilkinson & Harry Macdivitt
Axia Value Solutions Ltd

Published 2017 by arima publishing

www.arimapublishing.com

ISBN 978-1-84549-708-8

Printed and bound in the United Kingdom

abramis is an imprint of arima publishing

arima publishing
ASK House, Northgate Avenue
Bury St Edmunds, Suffolk IP32 6BB
t: (+44) 01284 700321

www.arimapublishing.com

Praise for the Seven Challenges of Value...

"Many talk about value and value based pricing but very few have been successful implementing this. This book takes a very pragmatic and concrete view on how to go about this in reality and what the real issues are. This has become mandatory reading for all my sales team."
Jurgen Van Hoenacker – Executive Director - Sales, Marketing & Wealth Structuring – Lombard International Assurance S.A.

"The 7 Challenges of Value is filled with lessons that will help you and your company improve performance. By starting with the reminder that value only exists from your customer's point of view and continuing through a progression of steps to capitalize and monetize the value that your organization creates,
this handbook will be a wonderful tool for you and your team."
Kevin Mitchell, President – The Professional Pricing Society, Inc.

"The 7 Challenges of Value is an ideal template for taking the Value Sales journey and moving from a generic value proposition into a specific and opportunity oriented one, paving the way for your differentiation and the de-commoditization of your product and services."
Gustavo Raiter – Vice President Sales People Development – Ceragon Networks

"One of the biggest issues facing sales and marketing is in delivering the value the customer really wants, not the value you think the customer wants. The 7 Challenges of Value provides a formula for success with today's customer driven sales process where vendor selection is based primarily on delivering positive financial results."
Dick Orlando COO & President – Leverage Point Innovations Inc.

Who are we?

Mike Wilkinson's passion and major area of activity is Value and Value Based Selling. Mike has delivered training and consultancy events all over the world, predominantly in the B2B area focussing on Value Based Selling, Sales Management and Managing Major Sales. The primary challenge has been to address margin erosion and move sales teams and organisations away from a "discount default" and towards a greater value orientation.

Harry Macdivitt trains and consults on a wide range of marketing and business areas across the world. His passion is value and Value Based Pricing. He brings a wealth of experience in strategic marketing and management to his training – having worked in senior positions in sales, marketing and business development for the public sector, academic, manufacturing and services sectors.

Our aim is to help our clients to reach a deeper understanding of the value of the solutions they deliver to their customers and through that understanding enable them to differentiate, price and communicate their offer accordingly.

We would really like to hear from you about your experiences identifying, communicating and pricing your value. We would particularly like to hear from those with experience of implementing a Value Based Pricing approach – successfully or otherwise! So please contact us at info@axiavalue.com and visit the website at www.axiavalue.com

Table of Contents

Foreword

From Peter Thomson

But I can do it cheaper...

That's not what I want. I want a relationship. I don't just want to be one party in a transaction. So many business owners and their people fail to recognise this basic difference in the type of customer (or clients) who wish to engage with them and buy their products and services. 'Discount Default' rules the way they 'negotiate'. Though how they manage to call it negotiation I struggle to understand.

At last! Solutions are here. In "The Seven Challenges of Value" Mike Wilkinson and Harry Macdivitt set out a clear pathway to understand the true meaning of 'value' in the customer/supplier equation. The Value Triad© brings common sense to the party and Willingness to Pay (WTP) introduces a key concept missed by most in their preparation for the engagement.

The world is full of companies and individuals prepared to supply those we seek to attract to our businesses. They (the other suppliers) are often prepared to sacrifice long-term relationships for short-term profits as they load their advertising and marketing messages with vague-value statements and bulging bonuses.

Value – value above everything is what customers want. Sure, there are always going to be those for whom 'Price is Everything' and if you and I have decided to be in that market we'll deal with them - and stack it high and sell it cheap. Just look what happened to Woolworths! But for those with growth, customer satisfaction through value and the future of all stakeholders uppermost in their mind – then VALUE is the watchword they live by.

Delve deep into this apparently simple book. My second reading discovered ideas I'd missed the first time. It's a companion, a guide and a surprising source of inspiration to take everything to the next level – sprinkling real value, not just the word, into any and all communications and relationships. Thank you Mike.

Peter Thomson
Peter Thomson International
The UK's leading strategist on business and
personal growth

The Seven Challenges of Value

Introduction

Back in late 2010 we put together our book "The Challenge of Value". I'm not sure that at the time we fully realised just how timely it was or how many of the ideas within it would become mainstream views on interpreting and understanding value. The Value Triad© is now very much a part of value language – so thanks for that!

In the intervening period, we have not stood still. Value Based Pricing was published by McGraw Hill in 2012 and has become essential reading on many university and college degree courses and as a practical pricing handbook for those in business.

We have also continued with our speaking and conference work and have been lucky enough to go all over the world talking about value and value pricing.

The catalyst for the original book had been a conference in Copenhagen where the delegates had all said they sold value

– so I checked to find out what their understanding of value was. Unclear, to say the least, and from that our definition of value and the Value Triad© emerged.

Another Conference

The catalyst for this book has been another conference. A year or so ago I was speaking at an event when someone who had read our original Challenge of Value book came up to me for a chat. Happily, they loved the book (so if you haven't read it already you really should!) He just blew me away with the most obvious question I had simply failed to consider:

"I understand the challenge of value, but realistically there has to be several different value challenges. I just wondered what they are?"

The Obvious Question

How obvious is that?! Inevitably it set us to thinking, and over the next few months we started working on an answer to what became known, to us at least, as "The Obvious Question!" As the answers began to emerge we started testing them out and doing some background research to make sure we were on the right track. It's fair to say that the Challenges of Value have been through several changes to get where they are today. Not just changes in content but changes in number and changes in what to call them. Finally, since we had identified seven, and they were challenges of value we called them:

The Seven Challenges of Value.

The Value Journey

As time goes by, no doubt some more will emerge and some will change. Please, don't just feel free but positively encouraged to get in touch with us to discuss your experience of value and especially how you feel about the 7 Challenges. From both a sales and an organisational perspective we believe they take us on a logical value journey from value discovery at one end of the process to value delivery at the other. In some ways it's simply a means to understand the value challenges that people and businesses face on that journey. In another it provides a valuable strategic and practical framework to help understand and develop the value that our customers are looking for.

Whether you are in sales or in marketing, or indeed anywhere in the business, it's a great way of looking at value and helping to overcome the challenges and deliver real value to customers.

In a world where margins and profits are under ever increasing pressure and the temptation to discount to win precious business is seemingly always there, there has never been a more important time to understand and deliver real value. But what is real value?

The Basic Business Challenge

In terms of challenge I start with something I call The Basic Business Challenge (or BBC for short!) This is the need to Understand, Create and Deliver value. In essence it is what all businesses are striving to do. However, there is one key element missing from this – the customer. Too many businesses define value from their own perspective and not from that of their customer. At a conference only the other week we were discussing the "Big Issues" of unleashing the power of value within business when one delegate came up with a brilliant statement:

"We think we know the value, only we haven't asked the customer."

"We think we know the value, only we haven't asked the customer..."

On that basis, the BBC fails to deliver and has the potential to take us in completely the wrong direction. It's time to upgrade the BBC to:

The Real Business Challenge

- Understand *Customer* Value
- Create *Customer* Value
- Deliver *Customer* Value

The 7 Challenges provides us with a guide to the things we need to consider in order to do this. We hope you enjoy the journey…

First, the 7 Challenges of Value:

Challenge # 1: Understanding just what value is.

Challenge # 2: Recognising that people's perceptions of value are constantly changing.

Challenge # 3: Identifying the people who care about your value.

Challenge # 4: Differentiating your offering.

Challenge # 5: Communicating your Value.

Challenge # 6: Capturing your value through price.

Challenge # 7: Delivering and measuring your value promise.

Whilst each of the challenges follows on from the previous challenge, it is also an iterative process. However, some of the challenges cannot be addressed until you have accepted and addressed previous challenges.

Challenge # 1:
Understanding just what value is

The first challenge that absolutely must be addressed is to develop an understanding of value:

So, let's start at the very beginning

A very good place to start

When you read you begin with A B C

When you sing you begin with Do Re Me

With value, you begin with.......

Value from whose perspective?

There really are two parts to this:

1. What is value as a concept? How do we define it and what are its component parts?

2. What does value mean to our customers? This is critical. There are often significant differences between what we see as value and what our customers perceive it to be.

Logically, to understand what value means to our customers we must start with a clear understanding of what value means to us.

This is often seen to be a very simple thing to do – a bit like defining quality! The problem is that most people define quality – and value – from their own perspective. Whilst you may know what great value looks like to you, to assume that it means the same thing to customers, or indeed anyone else, is a potentially serious mistake. Worse, perceptions of value change depending on situation and information. (see Challenge #2)

We define value from our own point of view and our customers define it from theirs. So, what do you think the chances are of both definitions being the same? That's it. Zero or thereabouts. And when you try to sell your view of value to people who take a somewhat different view to your own, the result is confusion. Especially if your customer isn't quite sure what value is either.

And what if your customers all define value slightly differently? How do you reflect this in your pricing? You could try to align perceptions in order to apply a coherent pricing framework, or you could respect individual value perceptions and end up with tailored pricing for each client (but having pricing inconsistency…). Either way is a challenge and how you address it will depend on the nature of your business and your customers.

Your customers understand value do they?

It's all very well selling based on value, but what happens if your customer has only ever really thought of value in terms of low price? Or you are talking to people in the customer organisation who appear to only want to talk to you about price? (These people are often referred to as Procurement! However, do not be misled. Professional procurement people are very aware of real value and its potential impact on their business. They are also well aware of the power of price). Either way, it's time for some education. And to do that you need to be able to calculate just what sort of an impact your solution might have on the customers' business and put together a compelling case. And you need to have the confidence to be able to deliver it.

The Dreaded "Discount Default"

One of the biggest challenges we find sales teams – and as a result businesses – trying to overcome is what we call the "Discount Default". This is the tendency to look to win business by discounting. Whenever any price pressure is applied, the reaction is to discount. However, this only plays into the buyer's hands. By discounting to win you are implying that there isn't any other reason they might wish to buy from you. Your potential value to the customer is ignored and price assumes the highest level of importance. However, just because something is the lowest price doesn't make it the best, or even the best solution.

> *"By discounting to win you are implying there's no other reason why the customer should buy from you..."*

It's not how little you pay, it's how much you get

Buyers will always tell you that you are too expensive – because to them you are! You need to move your focus away from price and towards your value. You need to develop enough confidence to be able to say to your customer: "No. When you look at the value we deliver we are far from too expensive. In fact, I would suggest we are not expensive enough!"

To be able to do that you need to accept and address "The Seven Challenges of Value."

Defining Value

So let's start with a simple definition of value. Over the years, we have seen literally hundreds of different definitions which simply goes to reinforce the view that everyone's perspective is slightly different. Given that is the case, the one definition that really seems to encapsulate the complexity of value in the simplest way is:

"Value is a Mystery"

This thought-provoking definition came from a group of chemical engineers in Copenhagen several years ago. For our purposes it is perfect. Value is a mystery and our job, both as businesses and as sales people, is to solve that mystery.

In our Value Sales Process, we consider this under Value Discovery (page 58).

However, solving the mystery is frequently a challenge in itself. It calls for a wide-ranging approach that includes input particularly from marketing at the segment level and sales at the customer level. This doesn't mean we are unlikely to have a good idea of the sorts of things potential customers might value. If you have been in business for any length of time you begin to understand the sorts of things that customers do want – that's both a help and a hindrance.

Generic Value and Specific Value

These are the terms I use to help differentiate two important concepts:

Generic value is the value that all businesses operating in the same business segment are more than likely to be looking for. Your experience tells you that each business in a particular segment has the same or similar challenges and, as a result the same overall requirements. For example, it's probably safe to assume that if I'm talking to sales directors/V.P.'s they all face similar issues – margins under pressure, sales force selling on a discount default, sales cycle times lengthening etc. Like all assumptions, these should be checked out with the customer to make sure they really apply to them, but the chances are it would be safe to prepare on the basis that these are likely to exist.

Specific value is different. It is exactly that, specific to the individual customer. Being part of a defined customer segment does not mean that every customer is identical. Every customer is unique and whilst they will have many challenges in common, there will be some that are specific to them and them alone. Often it is our ability to uncover these that is crucial.

So, there are two things that need to be done:

1. Check out whether your initial assumptions are correct and amend as necessary

2. Uncover the specific issues that apply to this customer

Once this is done you need to understand the relative importance that the customer places on these and whether the issue is big enough to motivate them to change.

The Value Triad©

Knowing that value is a mystery isn't entirely helpful without some idea of what actually constitutes value. What is required is some sort of value framework, and for that we created The Value Triad©.

The Value Triad© has two functional, tangible elements – Revenue Gain and Cost Reduction, and one intangible, but extremely important element which we call Emotional Contribution.

The Value Triad©

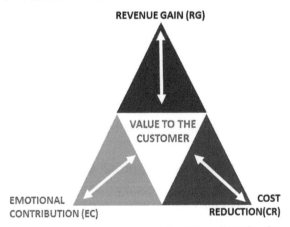

Source: Macdivitt, H., and Wilkinson, M. Value Based Pricing, McGraw Hill (2011)

Figure 1: The Value Triad©

The first two are, relatively, easy to understand.

Revenue Gains (RG)

Question to ask: How does my product or service help my customer to improve their revenue? (or performance if revenue is not a key measure i.e. patient outcomes in healthcare)

These are the improvements in revenue that accrue to the customer as the result of the purchase and use of your products and services. Outcomes such as superior yield from manufacturing processes or service delivery initiatives, greater revenue streams through their ability to create and sell a better and more competitive service, or through their ability to charge a premium price for products and services in turn, or to increase market share. They all generate revenue gains.

Cost Reduction (CR)

Question to ask: How does my product or service help my customer to reduce their costs?

This is our ability to help a customer to reduce his costs through the use of our products and services. This is not merely about reducing the price of purchased goods and services. Cost reductions for your customer can also be achieved by reducing direct labour hours, having longer periods between

> *...this is about cost reduction, not price reduction...when customers say they want you to reduce your price, what they really want is help to reduce their costs.*

servicing, employing less expensive personnel, training staff in new skills, reducing short and long term capital expenditure, and so on. Cost reductions must be achieved without compromising subsequent value delivery to your customer's customer. The key here is that this is about **cost** reduction NOT **price** reduction. The two are not the same thing. Clearly, if you reduce your price this will result in a cost reduction for the customer. But increasing your price and selling a better, more tailored solution may result in even better cost reductions for your customer. In virtually every case, when customers say they want you to reduce your price what they really want is for you to help them reduce their costs.

Emotional Contribution (EC)

Emotional contribution is something else. Much more difficult to put a number on but no less important. In fact, sometimes more important. Much more.

It's to do with the difficult to measure stuff like trust, confidence, risk reduction, brand image, feeling like you're the people they want to do business with. Not easy to measure, but all too easy to forget. So why do you sometimes pay more for things than you have to? Or buy from one store when the store down the road does the same things for less? Because the store is nicer, the staff are better informed, they treat you like a real person not an interruption to their day, you recognise the name over the door and it says good things to you. And guess what? B2B is really no different. No matter what they try to tell you!

So what now?

Now you must get out there and ask your customers what they really value. Once upon a time the focus was on identifying customer needs, then we had to find their pain points, then their challenges and their opportunities and so it goes on.

> *"Our customers define value, not us. If our customers don't see it as value, it's not value"*

These things are still important. But now we also need to understand the things they truly value, the things that help them and their businesses make money, save money and feel good about themselves. This is not as easy as it sounds. It should be, but it isn't.

You need to develop real confidence to ask the sort of questions that make your customers sit back and think. The one thing you really have to do is ASK! Ask your existing customers why they buy from you. Really. You will be amazed at what they tell you, and often the answers are very different from what you would expect – but then that's you defining value from your point of view and your customers defining it from theirs.

Ask your target customers what value looks like from their point of view. That way you'll be providing solutions that deliver the value the **customer** wants, not the value you **think** the customer wants.

For each customer, the "mix" of the three Value Triad© components will vary. For some customers, the focus will be on Revenue Gain, for others it will be Cost Reduction and others still Emotional Contribution. The key is to flex the Value Triad© to meet the specific requirements of individual customers and to develop and tailor your response accordingly. You will only be able to do that if you really, really understand the customer and the things that are important to them. How can you help them deliver more value to **their** customers?

Challenge # 2:
Recognising that people's perceptions of value are constantly changing.

Would you believe it? You find out in one meeting what the customer appears to value only to find out at the next one that it's all change! What is going on?

The problem is that people's perceptions of value change depending on location, situation, timing, state of mind, people, priorities, budgets etc. If they didn't, why would anyone pay £2.50 (and the rest!) for a Coke in an hotel when it's only 40 or 50p in a store? In a word – or three ...location and situation.

I resent paying £2 for a bottle of water in a motorway service station, but how much would you pay for a glass of water if you were in the desert dying of thirst?

Here perceptions are changing as a result of location and situation.

The Price of a Watch – Changing Perceptions in Action!

When my daughter left university, she went to work at a high-class jewellery store as she thought about what she really wanted to do. I gave her a call after her first day to find out how she had got on. "The prices are disgraceful", she told me. "The cheapest watch in the building is £250 and we stock watches up to £10,000. £250 for a watch is a disgrace at any time, never mind when times are hard".

A month later she was at our house for dinner. During the evening she turned to me and said "Whatever you do, make sure I don't buy a watch from my store". I suggested that that seemed unlikely given her views about how extortionate the prices were. "Well, to be honest", she said "I did think that £250 was a lot for a watch to start with, but now I realise it's actually not very expensive at all!"

So it's cheap now is it??

"What? – How come they were extortionately priced a month ago, but now they're cheap?" The answer, of course, is changing perceptions. When she first started, she compared the £250 watch with the watch that she was wearing – a very cheap, functional student watch costing a few pounds. Compared with that, the £250 watch was expensive. A month later and she's now comparing the £250 watch, not with her cheap watch, but with the £10,000 watches she also sells – compared with them £250 is cheap!

So, when you – or your customers – compare your prices, are you comparing them with the student watch or a top of the range £10,000 version? It makes all the difference to perceptions.

Buyers will frequently compare your proposed solution with a competitor and try and convince you the offers are identical. But are they? Don't forget that the customer is usually buying far more than just a product. They are buying the whole experience of dealing with you and your company. The product is just a component of the total package. If you lose sight of that you are in danger of a feature by feature comparison of your product against another and that usually leads nowhere good!

Willingness to Pay (WTP)

There is a danger that the customer may well have formed an opinion of our product or service before even hearing our offer. This opinion may be incorrect, but it will have established a "Willingness to Pay" (WTP), based on potentially erroneous information or invalid comparisons.

We call this the "Uninformed WTP hurdle" and it is a frequent and serious issue. For businesses and salespeople, if you don't have a good answer to why the customer should pay more for your product or service than they would for a competing solution you run the risk of price being the only differentiator and that moves you straight back into "discount default" country.

From Uninformed to Informed

Figure # shows the impact of moving the customers Willingness to pay from "Uninformed" to "Informed". Without selling any more in terms of volume, the move can have a very positive impact on revenue whilst at the same time satisfying the customer more effectively.

In Uninformed Willingness to Pay there are often one of two things happening:

1. The customer genuinely doesn't understand the full capabilities of your solution and the positive impact it can have on their business. As a result, our job is to first of all fully understand the issues and challenges they are trying to address and then help them appreciate the benefits and value of our approach and the positive impact we can have on their business.

2. Some customers, on the other hand, know full well what benefits your solution will deliver but want to focus on price. Maybe they do understand the value but just want to put pressure on you to reduce

your price. If you don't fully understand the impact your solution can have on the customer's business defending your price becomes more difficult.

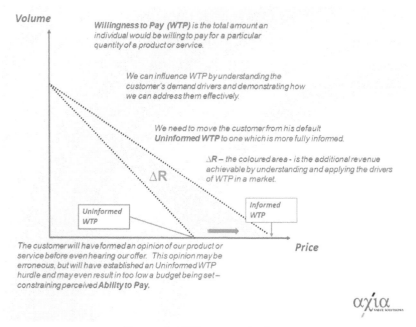

Figure 2: Willingness to Pay

An Example

Imagine I sell apples. You have a choice of two, both of which look very much the same. If you knew that one of my apples was hand-picked this morning and was organic would this information encourage you to pay a premium? I'm sure some of you are thinking "Yes, I would. I prefer to know where my food comes from and that it is wholesome". Others of you will be thinking "No way! I'm not interested in that, just give me the cheapest." Your customers are just the same. They define value from their perspective too.

They also define value dependent upon the information they have available. For example, if my apples look exactly like the apples next to them that were grown months ago on the other side of the world, were sprayed with pesticides to keep the bugs at bay, have been shipped from one side of the world to the other, been held in cold store for weeks and have only now arrived on the shelf of your local supermarket why would they pay more for mine?

Unless we provide them with information that helps them to make their decision, that moves them from an Uninformed Willingness to Pay to an Informed Willingness to Pay they won't. Why would they? I have failed to provide any sensible reason or argument for them to do so and failed to differentiate my apples in any meaningful way. This is part of the answer to the customer's question "Why should I choose you?"

> *"Understanding your customers is at the heart of value selling"*

But imagine how much easier life would be if we already knew those customers who were interested in fresh, organic products. Understanding your customers is at the heart of selling on value.

So, what can you do to make sure that customers understand and recognise your value?

The starting point is to understand and recognise the customers value requirements and drivers. This stems from a deep and critical understanding of the customer. Later in the book we take a look at a Four Step Value Selling Process (page 58). The Value Discovery component is the key to unlocking customer value drivers and influencing Willingness to Pay.

If you relate the elements of the Value Triad© to this it helps:

1. **Revenue Gain** – if you want to demonstrate how your solution can deliver revenue improvements you need to understand how your customer generates revenue. Who are their customers? How do they segment their customers? How do they deliver value to their customers? How can you help them do that better and help them create greater value for their customers? (so that their customers are prepared to pay a premium for the additional value)

2. **Cost Reduction** – if you want to demonstrate to your customer how your solution can help them to reduce their costs you need to understand exactly where they generate costs. In detail. We frequently come across a real lack of understanding in this area. If you don't understand where your customer incurs

cost it is going to be very difficult to demonstrate your ability to help them save cost. The risk is that all you will have to fall back on is meaningless platitudes – we can help you save money. Everyone says that, you need to be different and be able to say how much money you will help them save and by when.

3. **Emotional Contribution** – this is about the people. It doesn't matter how good your solution is, if you haven't got the people on board you haven't got anything. This is about making sure that everyone involved in the purchase decision sees you as a viable partner who they can trust, feel comfortable with and generally makes them "feel good" about the decision.

Challenge # 3:
Identifying the people who care about your value.

Want to talk price? Talk to procurement. Want to talk value? Well maybe procurement are not quite the people you should be talking with. They don't *really* care about value, they care about getting the best deal, and that usually means a focus on price. (OK, if you're in procurement you might well disagree – if you're in sales that's just how it feels!) The solution is to find people in the business who care about value and, particularly, your value. (but you'll need to understand what value is before you can really do this! See Challenge #1)

Making sure you're talking to the right people when you want to communicate and sell based on your value is key. A real-life example makes the point.

Talk to the Right People!

One of our clients is a large provider of Business Information (BI) software. Historically they had sold, or tried to sell, their sophisticated software to the logical buyers in their target customers, the IT department. Results were not encouraging. Not only were they struggling to get buy-in to the solution they provided, they found themselves outside the IT departments budget too!

We asked them what they were selling – the answer was software. We then asked them what their customers, the real customers, the people who actually benefited from what they did, were buying.

The answer? - The ability to make top level business decisions based on accurate and timely information. So where did the IT department fit in? Other than as the people who would manage the service, they didn't. The people who would benefit were top level managers and board members. Once they started talking to these people and they began to appreciate how much the software and access to great BI could help them, budgets become more readily available and orders began to flow!

> *"Talk to the people who will benefit from your value"*

Talk to the people who will benefit from your value....

In looking at gaining access to any new or existing client, the goal should be to talk to those people who will appreciate the benefits, and the value, of the solution you provide. Sales people constantly discuss how high up in an organisation they should try to gain access. A good starting point is to ask yourself, "Who benefits the most from the real value our solution could deliver?" and start there.

There is another very good reason for talking to the people who benefit the most from your value. If you get them on your side and excited about what you can do, they can then become, potentially, your internal sales people. This is sometimes referred to as the coach but I think these people offer a little bit more. Whatever they are called they will often help you navigate the complexities of their buying process, helping to identify the key people, who you need to see and what will bring them on board.

However, I think over the years I've made another discovery.

> *"The buying decision is frequently made when the seller is not there"*

For most sales people, especially those selling complex products and services, the final decision to buy from your company is often taken when you aren't there. That's right. The decision to buy is rarely taken with a seller sat in front of the buyer. This means two things:

The "Who" and the "How"

1. You really do need to understand not just the "who" but the "how". Knowing the who is only part of the job. You really need to make sure that you, or an appropriate colleague has been in touch with everyone and has done their utmost to bring them onside. This is what I call "Covering the Bases".

    The "How" is also crucial. I often find there is a reasonable understanding of who is going to be involved in the decision, but much less clarity on the how. This is a mix of the "who" and the "how". Who will make the decision – will it be a group decision where everyone votes? Will it be one person taking advice from others/ (if so, who is involved in the process?) Don't just ask one person how the decision is going to be made, ask a number. That way you are more likely to end up with a true picture of what is going to happen.

2. You need to know how you can support those people who benefit the most from your value. These people will, in essence, be representing you in the meeting. Have you provided them with all the help and support they need to represent you effectively? Are

you confident they will do a great job for you? Are you sure it really is you that they want to win? Are they held in high regard by their colleagues – in other words do their views and recommendations carry enough weight?

In talking to each of these people it is important to build up a picture of what value looks like to each of them. Even though they all work for the same organisation, each will see things differently from each other. Finance people will see things with a finance hat on, operations with an operations hat, production with their hat etc. The Value Proposition you deliver to each of them should take this into account and demonstrate how your value addresses their specific requirements as well as the broader company requirement. More on Value Propositions later!

Challenge # 4:
Differentiating

The first thing to know about differentiation is that being different isn't necessarily differentiation. I have a silver coloured car. I could have had the same car but in white. That's different – it's not silver! But I didn't want a white car. The difference was of no value to me because I didn't really care one way or the other. What I did care about was fuel economy and that was a difference to which I did attach a value. So, a car that could do significantly greater mpg would have a difference that I valued (all other things being equal).

That's differentiation – being different in ways that your customer truly values. So, you need to understand value and you need to understand your customer's perception of the things they value.

> *"Being different is not differentiation. Differentiation is being different in ways the customer values"*

Get out of the commoditisation straightjacket...

In many ways, the opposite of differentiation is commoditisation - something becomes commoditised when one offering is virtually indistinguishable from another. Buyers frequently try to persuade us that our product or service is identical to a competitor's; therefore, the only thing we need to talk about is price. More worryingly, many sales people come to believe it!

In our experience, very few companies actually sell commodities; there is always room for some differentiation – service levels, relationships, payment terms, stockholdings etc. But remember, any of these is only a differentiation if our customer sees it that way – in other words, sees the value. (Check Challenge # 1 – just what is value? Check Challenge # 2 – Value perceptions change. Check Challenge #3 – you need to be talking to those people who appreciate your value!)

Create an approach to differentiation

So, we need to create a differentiation strategy which has several strands:

1. Really understanding the things that our customers value (back to Challenge #1). If you have segmented your market, you can look for differentiators firstly at a segment level, and then tailor these to the specific

needs of individual customers within the segment. The more you can develop and communicate a differentiation that your customer really values, the less inclined they are likely to be to investigate competitive alternatives.

2. Understanding the strengths and weaknesses of our competitors (what do we need to know about our competitors? Everything!) Inevitably there will be some things that your competitors do that they might do better than you, and vice versa. Your job is to make sure that the things you do best are the things the customer values the most! This

> *"What do you need to know about your competitors? – Everything!"*

area is frequently a weakness – we like to think we know the competitor but the reality is we don't. Make sure you spend time getting to know and understand everything you can about your competitors – and their people. What do you need to know about your competitors? - Everything!

3. Recognising our capabilities and focussing on those areas where we can develop a real edge – what can we do better than our competitors and that is highly valued by our customers? In understanding our

customers value drivers in detail, we can ensure that we stress our strengths around those areas that add the greatest value.

4. Developing a way of effectively communicating our differentiation (see Challenge # 5)

5. Capturing a share of the value of our differentiation through price (see Challenge # 6)

Areas of Differentiation

There are a number of areas of potential differentiation that you might like to consider (and loads of books on the subject!). For example, you could differentiate around:

1. **Your Product**. You may be fortunate enough to have a product that has a clear differentiation when compared with competitors. Don't forget though, that being different is not differentiation.

2. **Your Service**. The service you offer may be demonstrably superior to competitive offers

3. **Your people**. The people are all important. They are the people who understand, create and deliver the outstanding value you want to deliver to your customers. If they do those things better than the competitor, brilliant! Your people really do have the opportunity to be a key differentiator.

4. **Your company**. Some companies have an instant appeal and a brand image that attracts customers. If you are fortunate enough to work for one of them don't forget it is still your job to build on that good fortune and understand, create and deliver outstanding customer value.

5. **Your business segment**. It is possible that you have carved out a niche in an attractive customer segment where competitors are thin on the ground or simply not as effective as you are.

6. **Your product development/innovation**. Many companies look to their suppliers as sources of innovation. If you are seen as a key business partner this may well be part of your competitive advantage.

When you look at these, and other sources of differentiation, the thing they tend to have in common is that they are potentially transient. For example, if you have a great product that is clearly attractive to your customers, it won't be long before your competitors will copy it. If you offer great service and it is valued by customers, your competitors will attempt to copy that. If your people are your advantage you must keep investing in them to make sure they stay that way – and stay with you!

The key through all of this is to capture the value of your differentiation in your price. If you have differentiation that your customer(s) value, then it is appropriate to share that value. How much is shared will be the subject of negotiations and will be determined by the skill of your negotiators and their ability to demonstrate,

"You must know how your customer generates revenue and incurs cost"

monetise and communicate your value effectively (the Value Proposition will be key). The more you know about the things your customer truly values and the way their business works the better. As mentioned before, if you are going to demonstrate cost reduction and/or revenue gain, the more you know about how your customer generates revenue and incurs cost the better.

This leads us to Challenge #5...

Challenge # 5:
Communicating your Value.

Wouldn't it be a shame to spend time understanding the things your customer really values, speaking to the right people and creating a real differentiation, only to then fail to communicate your value effectively? Being different in ways your customer truly values isn't enough if the customer doesn't know about it. This is where a powerful and persuasive Value Proposition is crucial.

One of the tools we use to help understand and communicate value is:

The Value Hierarchy

Understanding your organisations capabilities and its overarching "value proposition" is important. However, we frequently come across businesses that either don't really have a corporate level V.P. or that effectively keep it secret. If you want to know whether you have one or not, ask one of the sales guys. If they don't know it, to all intents and purposes you don't have one!

We introduced this model in The Challenge of Value and subsequently in Value Based Pricing (McGraw Hill 2012). In a great many businesses, the Value Proposition starts and finishes at the customer level. This is because the sales team are the one group of people that customers look in the eye and ask "Why should we choose you?" The Value Proposition is, or should be the answer, tailored to the specific requirements of the customer in question.

The Value Proposition Hierarchy

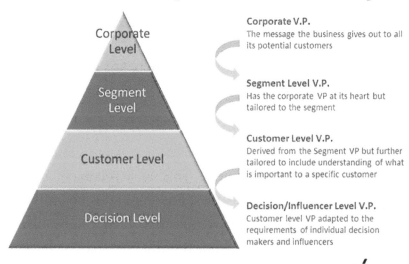

Figure 3: The Value Hierarchy

Each level of the hierarchy should begin the process of clarifying four key things for the customer:

- What product or service is your company selling?

- What is the end-benefit and value to me of using it?

- Who is your target customer for this product or service?

- What makes your offering unique and different?

> *"Your Value Proposition is your answer to the customer question "Why should we choose you rather than any other alternative?""*

As the Value Hierarchy name implies there are several levels:

Level 1: The Corporate Level V.P.

This is the top level message the business wishes to convey to all its potential customers. This is a relatively broad statement outlining what it does, how that adds benefit and value to customers and, where possible, what differentiates it from competitors. This is not the final persuasive reason why a customer should buy from you, that comes later.

In our experience the Corporate V.P. either simply doesn't exist or is so poorly defined as to be of little practical use.

Level 2: Segment Level V.P.

The segment level V.P. has the corporate V.P. at its heart (if it exists), but is tailored to the needs of individual business segments (how you define and segment your business is a different issue entirely and one that we will be addressing in a later book). Here the focus becomes a little sharper as the V.P. addresses more of the needs of those customers in each of your defined segments. So, for example, if you have segmented your business by industry you might have a segment for aerospace and one for offshore. The needs of each will be different and will be reflected in the Segment Level V.P. whilst incorporating the overall corporate message.

Level 3: Customer Level V.P.

Every segment is made up of a whole host of customers, each sharing similar characteristics, but each different in their own unique way. The task here is to take the Segment Level V.P. and tailor it to the specific needs of an individual customer. There are four primary sources of information to help in doing that:

1. **Your prospective customer** – this is your customer *as a business*. What are the key issues this customer faces, and what are the impacts on their business of these issues?

Value Proposition Drivers

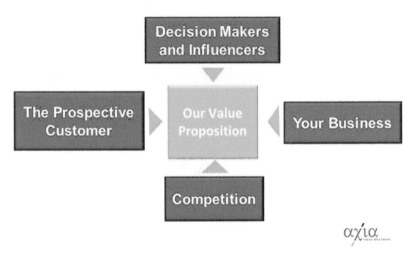

Figure 4: Value Proposition Drivers

2. **Decision Makers and Influencers**. This is your prospective customer – as individuals. Businesses don't make decisions, people do. What are the individual interests and motivations of each of the people who will be involved in making and/or influencing the decision?

3. **The competition** – whether we like it or not, it is unusual for there to be no competition. Sometimes the competition is the "do nothing option", or perhaps for the prospective customer to decide to do things internally. Don't forget the question – why should the customer choose you rather than doing nothing, or

doing things internally? How would they be better off choosing you?

4. **Your business** – Given your understanding of your customer, *as a business and as individuals*, the issues they face and the opportunities they have available, what can your company do to help? Particularly, what can your company do better than anyone else to add real value to the customer? How can you help the customer improve their revenues, reduce their costs and feel confident and comfortable dealing with you?

Whilst the Corporate Level V.P. might be put together by the board and the strategic marketing team, and the Segment Level V.P. might be put together by Product Management, the Customer Level V.P. is generally the province of sales. Indeed, in many businesses this is the only V.P. that exists and is generated on the hoof when the customer says "Why should we choose you!" This is not ideal.

Level 4: The Decision Maker/Influencer V.P.

Businesses don't make decisions, people do. In increasingly complex sales situations a wide range of people might be involved in the decision. Each will see things from their own point of view, their own perspective. This is the point where the Customer Level V.P. needs to be tailored to the specific interests of each individual. For example, the CFO will be interested in very different things to the COO even though they work for the same organisation. To be able to tailor your V.P. to each individual means understanding each individual, their corporate responsibilities and their personal goals. This calls for serious value discovery skills!

The value hierarchy looks at value starting with the overall promise your company makes to the market as a whole and ends with a focused, clear statement of the benefits – and value – a customer will get from dealing with you rather than choosing another alternative solution. Are you happy that you and your team are clear on the value you want to communicate? Do you have a clear Corporate Level V.P. and Segment Level V.P.'s? Do they help in putting together powerful, persuasive Customer and Decision Level V.P.'s? If not, are you making things more difficult for the sales team than they should be?

Finally, it's not an advertising strap line...

An advertising strap line is not a VP. "Saving our customers money"; "Delivering value everyday" "Because you're worth it!"

Neither is it a bland statement like "Our solution will save you money". This is little more than a vague expression of hope that most customers are likely to view with some scepticism

– especially since many of their other suppliers are likely to be saying the same things! Most of what passes for VP's are high on proposition and low on value.

Your VP should be powerful and persuasive, clearly answering a key question for the customer:

"Why should I choose you rather than one of your competitors?"

Powerful VP's are clear and to the point and clearly identify that you have understood the key issues and can deliver a demonstrable value.

"Our solution will save you money" – everyone tells me that!

"Our solution will save you $250k in the first year of operation by managing inventory and shelf life more effectively, and $200k a year in subsequent years."

When can you start?

I came across this wonderful tool some time ago. It really focusses your thinking on ensuring that your V.P.'s pass what is, effectively, a V.P. quality check.

The Value Proposition Framework

3 Components of Winning VP's

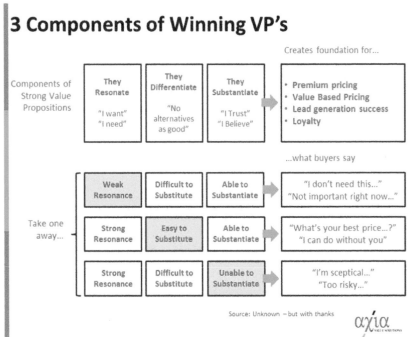

Figure 5: The Value Proposition Framework

There are three things the V.P. should do:

1. It should "resonate" with the customer. In other words, the customer should be able to clearly see how your solution will help to address their challenges and issues.

2. It should "differentiate" your solution from others. Whilst there may be other solutions that could do the job, nothing does the job as effectively as yours.

3. It "substantiates". You can clearly demonstrate your capability to deliver on your promise. This is normally through testimonials, case studies and the like. Frequently I find these are either not readily available or just not developed well enough. Case studies can be immensely powerful in convincing customers that you can do what you say you can do.

What is important to recognise is that a powerful and persuasive V.P. needs to have each of these components addressed effectively. Miss any one out and your V.P. is damaged, perhaps fatally.

Challenge # 6:
Capturing your value through price.

Value Based Pricing Defined:

"A value based price is designed and communicated such that all parties understand, recognize and accept the distinctive worth of products and services purchased in the transaction and participate optimally in the gains created by their use".

You'll find much more where that came from in our book *Value Based Pricing*!

That's easy for you to say...

Whilst as a definition it might not exactly trip off the tongue, the message is clear. Value Pricing is basing your price on the value you deliver to your customer. If you deliver no value, you don't get paid (or bought!), the more value you deliver, the greater your rewards. That, at least, is the plan.

However, if you don't understand or can't articulate your value, or you are dealing with a customer who can't or won't understand it, then you cannot sell or price on the basis of value. (See Challenge # 3) In those circumstances you fall back on price – you'll get the business if you're the cheapest. (Which, I'm assuming, is not part of the plan?)

Who said it was easy?

Value pricing is far from an easy option. You must have accepted – and met – the previous five challenges in order to be in a position to even consider doing so. And there is a huge amount of difference between wanting to value price and being able to do so. The other challenge is that implementation is an organisational issue. In our research for the book, Value Based Pricing, it became clear that basing prices on value means that the organisation as a whole must have a focus on creating real value for the customer. "This is a real leadership challenge. Top and senior management must be actively engaged and supportive...." We introduce a seven-part implementation framework in the book:

The 7 R's Framework

Having 7 Challenges naturally leads to having 7 stages to implement value across your organisation.

R1 – Recognise that change is necessary and why

R2 – Review current methods and readiness to change

R3 – Research and characterise customer value

R4 – Realign your company around value

R5 – Resolve opposition and reconcile genuine dissenters

R6 – Remove obstacles and roadblocks

R7 – Reward success

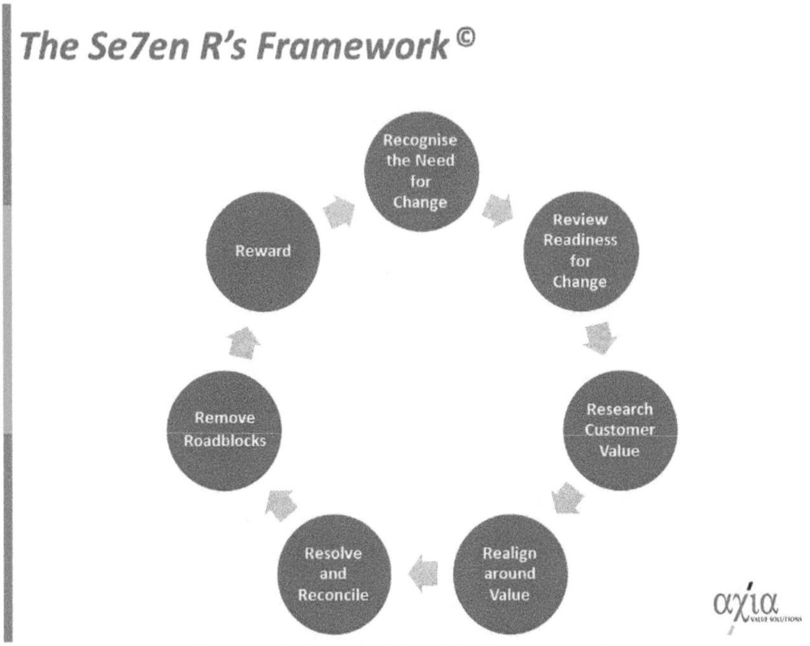

The Se7en R's Framework ©

Figure 6: The Se7en R's Framework

These are the steps in a little more detail:

1. **RECOGNISE** that change is necessary…

   Without real recognition of the need for change by business leaders, change will falter, fail or be flawed.

   "We need to get better business…"

   "We are better than this…"

   "Lifecycles are getting too short…"

   "We've got to stop margin erosion…"

2. **REVIEW** the way you currently go about pricing/ selling your products and services.

    If your methods are slack and undisciplined, you are leaving far too much on the table!

    "Our pricing methods are haphazard and random..."

    "Value? What's value??..."

    "Sales people seem to have forgotten how to sell..."

    "Death of a thousand discounts..."

    "All our buyers are price buyers..."

3. **RESEARCH** the value your customers want – and compare with what you are delivering.

    Is there a gap – and how big is it?

    "The only time we speak to customers is when they phone to complain..."

    "I've no idea how customers measure satisfaction..."

    "What is our value proposition? Today?"

    "Customers want solutions. We sell them products..."

4. **REALIGN** your business to customer value – bit by bit, one step at a time – and don't hurry it!

    "You guys have really improved..."

    "I trust you a lot more than the others..."

    "I like your value proposition..."

    "You are the best salespeople in our world..."

    "I get the chance to talk to you about our business..."

5. **RESOLVE** and reconcile genuine concerns tactfully, sensitively but firmly.

   Managers manage the business - the staff do not!

   "VBP is just a way to get sales people to sell higher prices..."

   "Why change things when they are working just fine?..."

   "VBP will help us all earn more..."

   "Let's all talk the value language..."

6. **REMOVE** obstacles and roadblocks. Apply the full range of change management disciplines and put this on a timeline...you are nearly there!

   "Everyone has a role to play in this work..."

   "I am glad you are keeping an open mind on this..."

   "Not every product is right for VBP but let's make it work on these..."

   "We want our partners to add value – not just shift boxes..."

7. **REWARD** everyone who has contributed to the success of the project.

   Have a party! Enjoy reaching the destination. Learn from the experience and incorporate that learning into the way you will do things in the future.

It is easy to assume that value pricing is the answer to all pricing problems. It isn't. It involves much hard work and the selection of the appropriate customers with whom to work. You cannot value sell and price to customers who are not prepared to have open discussions with you about the value they are looking for. Value customers are partnership customers. Similarly, you cannot have those discussions if those involved with dealing with your customers don't understand and/or cannot articulate the value you deliver. And finally, as we have seen, understanding and delivering value is an organisational issue – as we will see in Challenge #7.

However, we would make a clear distinction between Value Based Pricing and Value Selling.

Our definition of Value Based Selling:

"Value Based Selling is an approach to selling that aims to quantify the value that your solution delivers to a customer in economic terms, highlighting your advantages when compared with competing products or services".

Many of our clients operate based on published list prices. They cannot simply ditch them and change their entire pricing approach overnight. And an all-out VBP approach is highly unlikely to be appropriate. What the development of a highly skilled, value selling trained team is designed to do is to help justify your pricing based on the value you deliver. The inducement to buy becomes "value delivered" rather than just a discounting battle to see who cracks first.

This suggests that a key part of the sellers' role is educational (see the section on Willingness to Pay on Page 21). Customers won't be prepared or "willing to pay" anything unless they see real value for them in the purchase.

Once you have clearly identified the value drivers that are important to the customer, the next step is to demonstrate the extent to which you can deliver that value.

Challenge # 7:
Deliver and measure your value Promise.

Six Challenges down and one to go – the important one!

Ultimately everything that has gone before is little more than a promise. Yes, your promises should have been backed up with hard evidence that you can do the things you say you can do and can deliver the results. Wherever possible the results should have been monetised – so that your customers can see the "size of the prize".

Challenge # 7: Deliver & Measure your Value

Figure 7: Deliver and Measure your Value

A good starting point is to agree with the customer the value that you plan to deliver and to then measure the extent to which you are delivering against your plan. Having clearly defined KPI's in place from the start is an important part of the process.

If you are delivering your promise, make sure the customer knows about it. You will want to constantly reassure them that they are getting exactly what was expected – it helps to reinforce your credibility for the next sale. It will also provide you with an opportunity to create a case study that clearly demonstrates your ability to deliver what you say you will. Case studies can be very powerful ways of communicating your capabilities whilst at the same time building trust and reducing perceived risk.

However, if performance is not up to expectation you will need to know that as quickly as possible so that you can take steps to put things right. Again, you should share this with the customer to demonstrate that you are committed to their success.

Throughput the delivery process you will want to be looking for additional opportunities to deliver more value for the customer. You will want to deliver more insights as your knowledge of the customer and their business, their strategy and their opportunities grows.

Meeting the 7 Challenges of Value

To be able to meet the challenges a number of things need to be in place. For example:

1. Is everyone in the organisation clear about what value is? The Value Triad© provides a good template for beginning to explore an organisational understanding, but in moving to a value approach to business it is important that everyone in the business understands value, what it is, and what their role is in delivering it to the customer.

2. Is there an agreed Value Sales Process in place? We recommend a four-step approach. This is a simple approach which you should tailor to the specific requirements of your business/marketplace. You can also superimpose these steps on your sales pipeline to ensure that the right behaviours and activities are being undertaken at the appropriate time.

A Four Step Value Selling Approach

THE VALUE SALES PROCESS

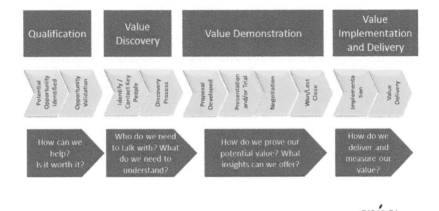

Figure 8: The Value Sales Process

(1) Qualification/Opportunity Assessment – before you go charging off in pursuit of every business opportunity that raises its head, you want to be sure it's going to be worth it. Do you have clear criteria in place for assessing whether an opportunity is worth pursuing or not? If you haven't you should. Far too much time is invested and lost in opportunities you either cannot hope to win or wouldn't want to. In particular, pursuing major sales opportunities can be an expensive business and you want to keep a firm hand on only pursuing those opportunities you can realistically be expected to win.

(2) Value Discovery – Value discovery is about much more than just needs analysis. It's about developing a real understanding of the business and the people in it, the challenges and issues they face, how they deliver value to their customers. This really is the critical part of the whole sales process – understanding customer issues and value drivers so that you can tailor your solution directly to their needs and demonstrate your value to them.

(3) Value Demonstration – once you have completely understood the customer, the time arrives for you to demonstrate how you can deliver great value to them. How can you differentiate your approach in ways that deliver demonstrable incremental value to the customer?

(4) Value Implementation and Delivery – up to now everything is the promise. Value delivery is the reality and it's really important that you measure how you are doing.

3. Has the Value Selling Process been effectively introduced, trained and coached? Having a process is one thing, having people apply it is quite another! In the projects we undertake this is a critical part of the process, and the coaching element is key. The reality that we have generally found is that in any reasonably sized sales team there are likely to be

some people selling on value already. They may not know it, but that is what they do, almost by default. There will then be a large number who will "get it" reasonably quickly and with help and encouragement will begin to apply it. There are also likely to be a few who, sadly, will never get it.

4. Have you identified the behaviours that are required for value selling to work effectively in your business? This gets to the heart of the question in many ways. To be able to measure the behaviours, you need to identify what the desired behaviours are in the first place. Do you have an up-to-date competency framework in place? Does everyone understand it? Is everyone happy that this reflects the organisations view of current best practice? Frequently we work with clients to identify what those competencies should be. Some examples:

- Great sales people ask great questions – so great communication skills all round is critically important

- Confidence – you can have all the skills in the world but if you don't have the confidence to apply them then nothing is going to happen. This is about providing people with the opportunity to try things out and build up their confidence. When you move from a "Discount default" approach to business to a "value default" it takes a good deal of courage to look buyers in the eye when they say you're too expensive and say "No we're not. When you look at the value we will deliver as a result of you doing business with us, I'm sure you'll see our price is highly competitive".

- They create and deliver powerful and persuasive value propositions – the answer to the customer's question "Why should we choose you rather than someone else?"

- Curiosity – if I was recruiting today, one of the things I would be looking for in someone is a natural curiosity. A real desire to know more, to ask great questions, to search out opportunities.

Once you have identified the full range of behaviours you can then start to think about how to measure them. The critical question is what you want the behaviours to achieve and start to measure whether they are, in fact, delivering those desired results. You should be clear that there is a direct correlation between particular types of behaviour and the results you are looking for. This provides two opportunities to measure performance:

a) By observation – are the sales team exhibiting the behaviours you desire. Are they asking great questions? Are they listening and summarising their understanding? Are they communicating value effectively?

b) By measurement – are the behaviours delivering the measurable results?

5. Do you have compensation mechanisms in place that reward the behaviours you need? The reality of reward mechanisms is that all too frequently they reward the wrong types of behaviour – and the things that get rewarded are the things that get done.

Starting the Value Journey

As with so many things, the real challenge is to get started! Addressing the Seven Challenges of Value applies to both individuals and organisations/businesses. Re-orienting a business around value is not an overnight activity. It requires determination and patience (See the 7 R approach on page 49).

Understanding, creating and delivering outstanding customer value is a team game. As a sales team or individual seller, you can begin to make a difference and become a "value evangelist" inside your business. However, to really win the Value Challenge you need to work as a team. If we can help on your journey, please get in touch.

At Axia Value Solutions we help our clients defend and grow their margins and build profitability. We do this by helping them to reach a deeper understanding of the value of the solutions they deliver to their customers and through that understanding enable them to differentiate, price and communicate their offer increasingly effectively.

Axia Value Solutions – Value through Understanding

For more information you can contact Mike and Harry at info@axiavalue.com *or click on the "Let's Talk" link on the website* www.axiavalue.com

List of figures

Lightning Source UK Ltd.
Milton Keynes UK
UKHW020639190620
365162UK00009B/76